MORE ABOUT JOHN AND HIS FRIENDS

Do you know John and his friends? John wanted to be like Mary, God's Mother. What story does the picture tell?

JOHN GETS right up when Mother calls. No dilly-dallying! He says his morning prayers and goes right in to breakfast. He eats all his breakfast, too, and does not have to be coaxed.

JOHN GOES to bed when it is time, and he does not fuss about it. He says goodnight to Mother and Dad.

JOHN WASHES up. He has hung up his clothes. What did he do with his books and toys?

JOHN SAYS good night to God and our Blessed Mother. He says: "Jesus, I love You. I tried to do what You want, all day long. I tried to be like you, Blessed Mother Mary. I love you so much. Please help me to keep on trying."

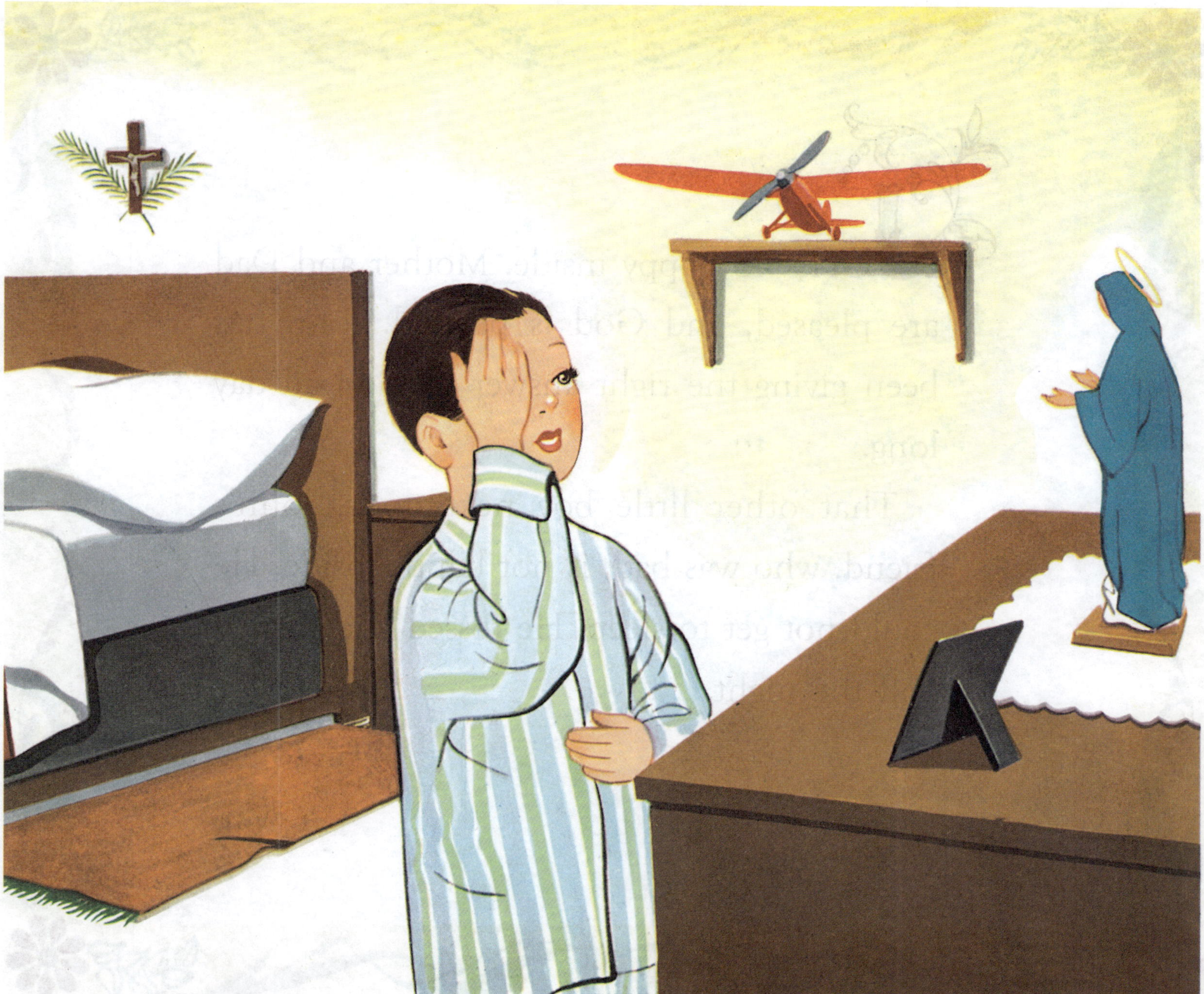

JOHN IS happy inside. Mother and Dad are pleased, and God is pleased. John has been giving the right answer to God all day long.

That other little boy next door, John's friend, who was bad, is not happy inside. He could not get to sleep. He tossed and turned half the night.

M
M

THIS IS that little girl, John's friend. I don't know her name. She was bad, and she is not happy inside. But she knows God loves her anyhow. She says: "Dear God, I'm sorry. I'll try to do what You want tomorrow. I want to be like Mary, our Blessed Mother." Then she felt happy inside and went to bed.

GOD WANTS all of us to be like Mary, our Blessed Mother. He wants every boy and girl in the whole world to be like her.

What can we do, to be like Mary?

We must always give the right answer, "I will do what God wants."

NOW FOLD your hands and close your eyes. God is listening. Whisper: "I want to be like Mary, our Blessed Mother. If John can always give the right answer, so can I. I will always try to do what You want, dear God. Please help me."

WUPSY PAYS A VISIT TO HEAVEN

One evening, Father George was saying his prayers outside his hut, and Sunny was sleeping peacefully. Wupsy looked up to a silvery moon that was already peeking from behind the clouds, and suddenly he knew, as Angels do, that God was calling him. It must be important, for God was using the beautiful long name that no one else could pronounce.

At once flew up high above the little round of Matongu, high above the great of the forest, higher even than the far off on the horizon. Soon the world looked like a great spinning slowly around. On the way up to Heaven he flew past and and lots and lots of and hundreds and hundreds of going and with messages. They were taking things to Heaven and bringing things to the . They each had a particular job to do. There were Guardian going up to report, there were Arch bringing special messages to and There were called Principalities who look after big cities, and some called Powers whose special job it is to deal with very troublesome . said hello to them all as he passed, and in less than no time he was in Heaven.

He first met crowds of other that he had known before he became a Guardian . " , ," they called, "tell us about ." But smiled and told them they would have to wait awhile, as he had to go straight to God about something. On he flew, past the wise Cherubim, who were very important

 , on to where the Seraphim were shining like great 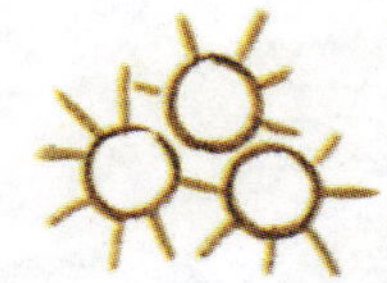 , on to where the Thrones serve God on His mighty throne. As he came near to God, 's  trembled with great joy and happiness, and he poured out all his love for God. Then he knelt down, bowing very low among the Thrones, with the great Seraphim shining like  and almost burning all around him. He felt very awed at being so near God, and yet not a bit shy.  are never shy with God.

 looked at God, and God spoke to him. God did not use words, but  knew at once all that God was telling him. God told him many things that he was very glad to hear. First of all, God explained how the  had prayed to the Guardian  and how the 's own  had brought his prayers to God. It was a good prayer, and God was going to grant it, but He wanted to grant the prayer through the Guardian . So He had chosen  to be a Guardian  to manage everything. Without knowing this,  had done just what God wanted him to do, which made him very happy.

Then God told him a lot about Sunny. God told Wupsy he must take very good care of Sunny, for He wanted him to be a priest some day like Father George. Then he could say Mass and hold God in his hands and forgive people their sins. But Wupsy would have to be careful because some day the devils would guess this, and stir up lots of trouble. God told Wupsy other things too, which were secrets between Wupsy and God and which made Wupsy very happy.

Wupsy was so pleased and happy that he could hardly keep from dancing right there at the very throne of God. He praised and thanked God as hard as he could, until finally he had to make way for other Angels who also wanted to come to the throne of God.

Wupsy went off to see the other Angels who were so interested in what he was doing. He told them all about Sunny and the new mission at Matongu, and even about the devils. Having always been in Heaven, these Angels had not run across a devil, and they were quite excited.

Wupsy stopped, too, to see some of the Angels who were called Powers. He wanted to get advice about the devils who try to stop boys from becoming priests. The Powers told him that there are ever so many big, powerful devils who do nothing else, for it is a very important job for them! Wupsy was warned of all the different things these devils might try to do: they would try to make Sunny die young, which made Wupsy tremble all over; then they might tempt him to do awful things like being proud and mean. They might set the witch doctors on him. They might try to make him homesick after he had started school, and they might tell him about all sorts of things that would seem to be more fun than being a priest. It was pretty frightening, and Wupsy was quite flustered. But the Powers said he need not worry, as God would help him to look after Sunny. Nothing could happen if Sunny always obeyed.

This was true enough; but it worried Wupsy, so he went back to the throne of God. There he knelt down in a quiet corner where he would not be in the way and prayed as hard as he could for little Sunny.

After that he felt much happier and set off for Matongu. It was getting darker now, and Wupsy felt very pleased when he saw Father George still sitting quietly outside his hut. Father was smoking his pipe and thinking. Wupsy knew that he was planning the new mission. He was making up his mind just where to put the church and his house. He was thinking of the catechism classes he would soon start.

Wupsy was even happier when he finally caught sight of Sunny sitting in front of his hut. He seemed to be listening to the soft night noises of the forest and watching patches of moonlight. So Wupsy quietly folded his Angel wings together and settled himself close beside Sunny and sent a prayer to God: "Thank You, God, for the good news today about my little Sunny being a priest some day. I promise to watch over, guard, and protect him. And thank You, God, for sending the missioners who will help keep Sunny's soul bright and shiny. Good night, God."

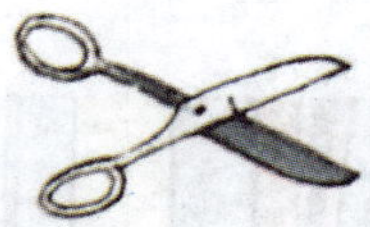

DOLLHOUSE CLEANING

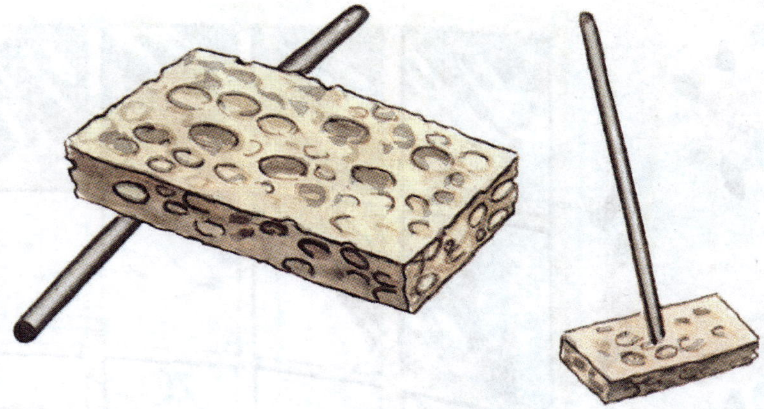

Lady Doll is just as particular about keeping her house clean as any other lady. Make what she needs to clean house.

A MOP: A piece of old sponge and a lollipop stick make a good mop. Cut an oblong piece of sponge. Make it look something like a tiny brick. Then put a small hole in the center by sticking a nail through it. Some glue on the end of the lollipop stick will hold it in the hole.

A FEATHER DUSTER: Feathers and a toothpick will do. Collect some feathers or short pieces of yarn, and tie them tightly to the end of a toothpick.

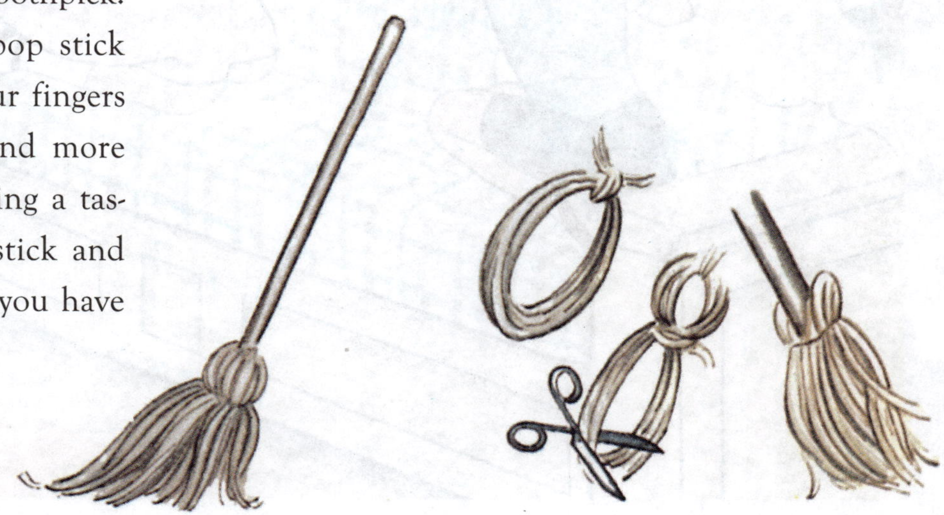

A DUST MOP: Some string and a lollipop stick are all you need. Loop the string around your fingers about ten times. Tie the loop and then wind more string around the middle of the loop, forming a tassel. Carefully glue the end of the lollipop stick and stick it into the top of the tassel. And there you have a nice little mop.

RAIN SONG

When drops of rain beat on the pane
I watch the raindrops racing.
It's always fun to see them run
And watch their game of chasing.
Outside, the green looks fresh and clean,
The roofs and pavements glisten,
And, drip-drop-drip, the raindrops slip
From roofs and branches. Listen!
I like their tune. But all too soon
The world looks wet and wetter.
Stop raining, rain, and leave again–
We do like sunshine better!

WHY SHOULD *I*?

Once there was a little girl named Molly, who had brothers and sisters and kind parents who loved her. She had enough to eat and pretty clothes, her own bed to sleep in and her own toys. In all, she was a very lucky little girl.

Molly did not seem to know that. She was forever complaining. "Why should *I* always have to dress Kathy? What can't Nan do it?" "Why can't *I* get a new dress, like the Babson twins?" "Why should *I* pick up the paper? I didn't throw it down!" "Why should *I* go to bed if Fred doesn't have to? He always gets things, just because he is older." "*I* can say the lines much better than Evelyn, why can't *I* have the part in the school play?"

Every day Molly became more and more unhappy and felt more and more sorry for herself. One day she felt so miserable that she decided to run away. She packed a few things into her doll's suitcase and quietly left the house.

A long way from home she bumped into somebody. Oh dear, it had to be somebody who knew her! Mrs. Henry, who cleaned most of the houses in the neighborhood, spoke to the little girl.

"My, my!" she exclaimed, "fancy meeting you here this hour of the day! You didn't get lost, did you?"

"No," said Molly, hoping she would not ask any more questions.

But Mrs. Henry was worried.

"Does your mother know you are here?"

Molly shook her head.

"Goodness, gracious me! She will be worrying herself sick. Better run home quickly."

"Why should I?" said the little girl, as fiercely as she could with a lump in her throat.

Mrs. Henry glanced at the suitcase.

"You didn't run away, did you?"

"Why shouldn't I?"

Suddenly Molly started crying.

"Why shouldn't *I* get a dress like the Babson Twins? . . . Why should *I* always dress my baby sister? . . . Why should Evelyn get the part when everybody knows I read much better . . .?"

All of Molly's worries came spilling out while tears rolled down her cheeks.

"My, my!" sighed Mrs. Henry. "I never knew that children, too, have so much trouble with that Commandment!"

"What Commandment?" Molly did not quite know what Mrs. Henry was talking about.

"The commandment that says: *Thou shalt not covet thy neighbor's goods.* It isn't always easy not to envy one's friends and neighbors. Of course, envy isn't stealing, but it is wrong all the same, and makes it people very miserable. I used to grumble myself, 'Why should I have to wear old clothes when the people where I work are all dressed up?' 'Why should I have to clean up after other people?' 'Why should I have to get up early every day?'"

The little girl looked at Mrs. Henry's hands, which were worn from washing other people's floors and dishes.

"Why don't you run away?" she asked.

"Goodness, gracious me, what a question!" laughed Mrs. Henry. "No, little one, we all have to stay in our own place in life. Running away won't make us happier. But envying other people won't make us happy, either."

"Mrs. Henry talks as if I were grown-up!" thought the little girl proudly. But she found it hard to follow.

"You know what helps me?" asked Mrs. Henry. "When I have to do a job now, I don't ask, 'Why should I have to do it?' I simply tell myself, 'Nobody likes doing it, but it has to be done, and somebody will have to do it. So why shouldn't *I* be that somebody and try to do a good job?' Things don't seem half so bad that way. Try it sometime, when you have to help with the dishes.

"Instead of saying, 'Why shouldn't I be in the play?' you could say, 'It's much harder for Evelyn to get a chance, because she doesn't read very well. She wanted the part just as much as I did. Only one of us could be in the play, so why shouldn't I be the loser? I have so many things to make up for it.'

"And instead of spoiling the twins' fun by complaining that you didn't get a new dress, you could tell them how pretty they look in theirs."

"It's funny how you make things look the other way around!" said Molly. "But I'll be glad when Kathy is old enough to help with the dishes. And I still wish I had a dress like the twins."

"Of course you do," agreed Mrs. Henry. "We all wish for things. And maybe they will come true, if we work hard. It's only when we *envy* other people for the things and the time and fun *they* have, that we don't see all the good things *we* have! Then we become so miserable that we want to run away from the very place God wants us."

Molly certainly had a lot of new things to think about now. Suddenly she spoke up: "I think I'll go home for supper now. Besides, it's my turn to help with the dishes."

JACK'S HAT

If the players don't know each other's names, this is a good game for learning them. If they know each other well, they each choose a new name which the other players will have to remember.

An old hat (or cap) is used for "Jack's Hat." The player who starts the game takes the hat and calls: "Jack has lost his hat–Jimmy found it!" While he says "Jimmy found it," he throws it to Jimmy, who catches it and immediately answers: "I didn't find it–Mary found it!" while throwing the hat over to Mary. Mary has her answer ready: "I didn't find it–Bobby found it!" she calls, throwing the hat to Bobby on the far side of the circle.

And so "Jack's Hat" travels on from one player to the next. You never know who the next will be. It is very important to pass the hat quickly, and, of course, one has to call the right name while throwing it to the person of one's choice. Anybody who gets mixed up gets an invisible Dunce-cap for his mistake! When all the names have become familiar, the players can choose new names–or switch to a different game.

DARING DEEDS

The little wall by the garden hedge–
That's where I walk, quite close to the edge.
I have to be careful, for if I stumble
And lose my balance, I'll certainly tumble.
And Daddy tells me that, if I do,
I'll be Humpty Dumpty number two!